Riding Freedom

by
Pam Muñoz Ryan

Teacher Guide

Written by
Monica L. Odle

Note

The Scholastic Signature paperback edition, © 1998 by Pam Muñoz Ryan, was used to prepare this guide. Page references may differ in other editions. Novel ISBN: 0-439-08796-1

Please note: Please assess the appropriateness of this book for the age level and maturity of your students prior to reading and discussing it with them.

ISBN 1-58130-863-9

Copyright infringement is a violation of Federal Law.

© 2005 by Novel Units, Inc., Bulverde, Texas. All rights reserved. No part of this publication may be reproduced, translated, stored in a retrieval system, or transmitted in any way or by any means (electronic, mechanical, photocopying, recording, or otherwise) without prior written permission from Novel Units, Inc.

Photocopying of student worksheets by a classroom teacher at a non-profit school who has purchased this publication for his/her own class is permissible. Reproduction of any part of this publication for an entire school or for a school system, by for-profit institutions and tutoring centers, or for commercial sale is strictly prohibited.

Novel Units is a registered trademark of Novel Units, Inc. Printed in the United States of America.

To order, contact your local school supply store, or—
Novel Units, Inc.
P.O. Box 97
Bulverde, TX 78163-0097

Web site: www.educyberstor.com

Lori Mammen, Editorial Director
Andrea M. Harris, Production Manager/Production Specialist
Suzanne K. Mammen, Curriculum Specialist
Heather Johnson, Product Development Specialist
Vicky Rainwater, Curriculum Specialist
Jill Reed, Product Development Specialist
Nancy Smith, Product Development Specialist
Adrienne Speer, Production Specialist
Lenella Meister, Production Specialist

Table of Contents

Summary 3

About the Author 3

Background Information 3

Main Characters 4

Initiating Activities 4

Vocabulary Activities 4

Four Sections 15
    Each section contains: Summary, Vocabulary,
    Discussion Questions, and Supplementary Activities

Post-reading Discussion Questions 21

Post-reading Extension Activities 22

Assessment 23

Scoring Rubric 24

Skills and Strategies

Thinking
Research, compare/contrast, analysis, brainstorming, predicting, pros/cons

Comprehension
Cause/effect, retelling

Writing
Letter, poem, short story, diary, essay, review the book, song

Listening/Speaking
Discussion, oral presentation, public speaking, teaching

Vocabulary
Definitions, parts of speech, synonyms, antonyms

Literary Elements
Setting, conflict, theme, characterization, point of view, resolution

Across the Curriculum
History—transportation, biography, Gold Rush, slavery, women's rights, politics; Science—horses, technology advancement, sight; Art—drawing, collage, diorama; Math—distance, speed; Geography

Genre: historical fiction

Setting: New Hampshire, Rhode Island, Massachusetts, and California in early to mid-1800s

Point of View: third person

Themes: courage, freedom, adventure

Conflict: person vs. society, person vs. person, person vs. self

Tone: candid, conversational, informative

Summary

Charlotte "Charley" Parkhurst was born in New Hampshire in 1812. After she is orphaned at a young age, she finds herself in an orphanage where she discovers her gift for working with horses. Charlotte escapes from the orphanage dressed as a boy and begins going by the name "Charley." She becomes a stable boy and then learns to drive a stagecoach for a kind man named Ebeneezer Balch. When gold is discovered in the West, she moves to California to drive stagecoaches there but suffers an eye injury when she is kicked by a horse. Although she has lost sight in one eye, she continues to drive stagecoaches and becomes known as "One-eyed Charley" because of the eye patch she wears. After purchasing her own property in California, Charley registers to vote—both of which she can do only because people believe she is a man. She becomes the first woman ever to vote in a presidential election. Her lifelong friend, Hayward, comes to visit her, fulfilling their childhood dream. Ebeneezer then comes to live with Charlotte on her California ranch.

About the Author

Pam Muñoz Ryan was born in California on December 25, 1951, and raised in the San Joaquin Valley. She considers herself to be "truly American," as she is the descendant of those with Spanish, Mexican, Basque, and Italian ethnicity. As a young girl, she loved to read and wanted to become a teacher. She earned her bachelor's degree at San Diego State University and became a teacher and eventually an administrator. While earning her master's degree at SDSU, she became interested in writing. Today, she lives in San Diego County with her husband, four children, and two dogs.

Ryan has written over 25 books for young people, including the award-winning *Esperanza Rising*. Her picture books include such titles as *Amelia and Eleanor Go For a Ride*, *When Marian Sang*, and *Mice and Beans*.

Background Information

Charlotte "Charley" Parkhurst is an American historical figure. She was born in New Hampshire in 1812 and died in 1879 in California of rheumatism and cancer. She was orphaned at a young age and drove stagecoaches after escaping from an orphanage disguised as a boy. She had an excellent reputation as a stagecoach driver. After moving to California, she lost sight in one eye, causing her to wear a patch while driving horses. Besides being famous for stagecoach driving, Parkhurst is also famous for being the first female to vote in a presidential election, which she did in 1868. As the book indicates, her true identity as a woman was not discovered until after her death. At that time, it was also discovered that she was a mother.

While the rough outline of Parkhurst's life is accurately represented in *Riding Freedom*, some of the dates have been changed for the purposes of the story. The story surrounding how Charlotte was orphaned and the people who helped her through the years is fabricated.

Main Characters

Charlotte "Charley" Parkhurst: young orphan girl who disguises herself as a boy, escapes from an orphanage, and becomes a famous stagecoach driver and the first woman to vote in a presidential election

Hayward: Charlotte's younger friend at the orphanage who is adopted before Charlotte escapes; keeps in touch with Charlotte throughout her life

Mr. Millshark: overseer of the orphanage

William: a young boy; Charlotte's nemesis at the orphanage

Vern: man in charge of the stables at the orphanage; helps Charlotte escape; former slave

Mrs. Boyle: the cook at the orphanage; doesn't want Charlotte to get adopted because she would lose her kitchen help

Ebeneezer Balch: stable manager in Worcester, Massachusetts; hires "Charley" as a stable boy and teaches her to drive a stagecoach for him when he moves his business to Rhode Island; a father-figure to Charlotte

James Birch and Frank Stevens: leave Rhode Island to start a stage company in California; talk "Charley" into joining them

Margaret: widow who tells Charlotte about land for sale and becomes her neighbor

Initiating Activities

1. Brainstorming: Write the word "Courage" in the center of the Attribute Web (see page 6 of this guide). Allow students to brainstorm a list of meanings of this word.

2. Research: Have students research facts about the real Charlotte Parkhurst on the Internet or in the library. Divide the students into small groups and allow them to share the information they learned.

3. Research: Have students research facts about driving stagecoaches in the nineteenth century. Have them draw pictures that show a stagecoach and/or some routes that stagecoaches used to take. They could also write a short report explaining the risks involved in traveling by stagecoach in the 1800s.

4. Prediction: Present students with the following list of words—orphan, disguise, horses, gold, injury, voting. Have them predict what they think the book will be about. Students can begin the Prediction Chart on pages 7–8 of this guide.

Vocabulary Activities

1. Part of Speech Race: Randomly select 20 vocabulary words. Give each student a list of the words and start a timer. The first student to correctly identify the part of speech for each word as it is used in the book is the winner.

2. Word Sort: Assign students 20 vocabulary words. Have students sort the words into different categories, including verbs, nouns, adverbs, and adjectives using the Vocabulary Chart on page 9 of this guide.

3. Definition Game: Divide the class into two teams. Present one team with a vocabulary word to define. If the team correctly defines the word, it receives one point. If the team answers incorrectly, the opposing team has a chance to define the word. Then the opposing team is allowed to define the next word. Play continues in this manner until time is up or a list of words is exhausted. Each correct definition receives one point. The team with the most points wins.

4. Word Spin: Assign a different vocabulary word to each student. The student must create a spinner about the vocabulary word. The spinner must be divided into six sections, including definition, part of speech, word used in a sentence, picture of the word's definition, synonym, and antonym. Using a brad, the student must connect a paper arrow to the center of the spinner. Place the vocabulary spinners in a reading center where students can study them.

5. Vocabulary Story: Divide the class into four groups. Give each group a list of 7–10 vocabulary words. The group must work together to write a one-page story that includes each of the vocabulary words as they are used in the book. Then the group will select one person to read its story to the class.

Attribute Web

Using Predictions

We all make predictions as we read—little guesses about what will happen next, how a conflict will be resolved, which details will be important to the plot, which details will help fill in our sense of a character. Students should be encouraged to predict, to make sensible guesses as they read the novel.

As students work on their predictions, these discussion questions can be used to guide them: What are some of the ways to predict? What is the process of a sophisticated reader's thinking and predicting? What clues does an author give to help us make predictions? Why are some predictions more likely to be accurate than others?

Create a chart for recording predictions. This could either be an individual or class activity. As each subsequent chapter is discussed, students can review and correct their previous predictions about plot and characters as necessary.

- Use the facts and ideas the author gives.
- Use your own prior knowledge.
- Apply any new information (i.e., from class discussion) that may cause you to change your mind.

Predictions

Prediction Chart

What characters have we met so far?	What is the conflict in the story?	What are your predictions?	Why did you make these predictions?

Vocabulary Chart

Noun	Verb	Adjective/Adverb	Other

Story Map

Directions: Add to the story map as you read the novel.

Setting

Problem

Goal

Episodes

Resolution

Characters _____
_____

Time and Place _____
_____

Problem _____
_____
_____

Goal _____
_____
_____

Beginning ⟶ Development ⟶ Outcome
_____
_____
_____
_____
_____

Resolution _____
_____
_____
_____
_____

Character Attribute Web

Directions: The attribute web below will help you gather clues the author provides about Charlotte in the novel. Fill in the blanks with words and phrases that tell how Charlotte acts and looks, as well as what she says and feels.

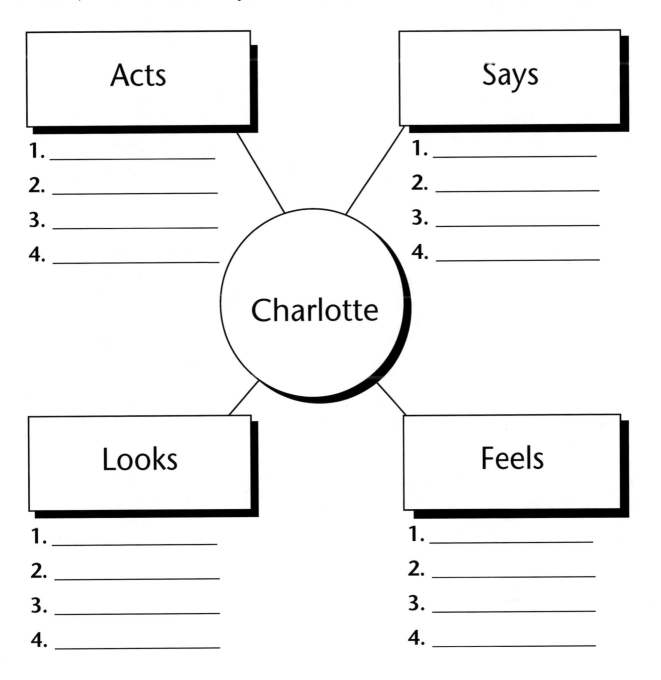

Venn Diagram

Directions: Think about how women were treated when Charlotte lived compared to how women are treated today. Complete the Venn Diagram.

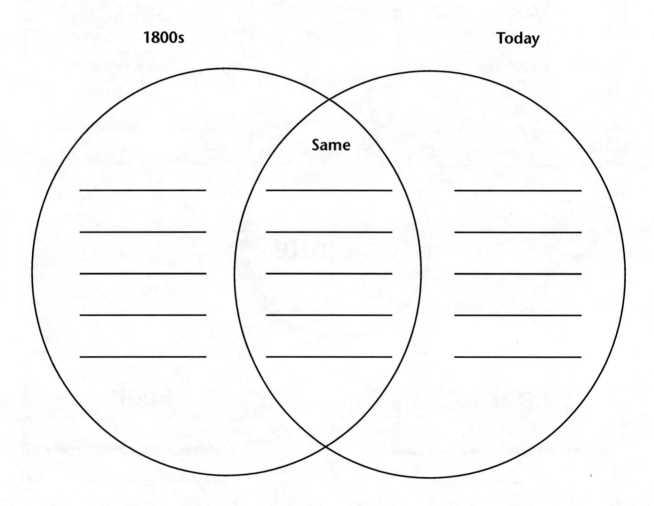

Who Am I?

Directions: Write a riddle describing a character in the novel. Include adjectives, adverbs, nouns, and verbs that will help other students see this character in their mind's eye. Describe how the person looks, acts, feels, talks, and how other people in the story treat this character. Have classmates guess the answer to your riddle.

Who am I?

I have _____

_____

_____

_____

I can _____

_____

_____

_____

In the story, people say I _____

_____

_____

Effects of Reading

Directions: When reading, each part of a book may affect you in a different way. Think about how parts of the novel affected you in different ways. Did some parts make you laugh? cry? want to do something to help someone? Below, list one part of the book that touched each of the following parts of the body: your head (made you think), your heart (made you feel), your funny bone (made you laugh), or your feet (spurred you to action).

Your head	Your heart

Your funny bone	Your feet

In the Beginning–Chapter 2, pp. 1–31

Charlotte "Charley" Parkhurst, a young orphan girl, loves to spend time with the horses at the orphanage where she lives. After her favorite horse dies, she is forbidden to ride anymore, and her best friend gets adopted. Charlotte decides to run away from the orphanage.

Vocabulary

blustery (2)
skittish (2)
harnesses (2)
ruffian (5)
plantation (7)
halter (10)
piercing (10)
lathered (11)
persistent (13)
foals (15)
filly (21)
stall (22)
notion (26)
bridles (28)
chaperon (30)
tendril (31)

Discussion Questions

1. What in Charlotte's past may have explained why she loves horses so much? *(When her parents were killed in a stagecoach accident, the horses stood next to her and protected her until help came. pp. 3–4)*

2. What does Charlotte enjoy about the orphanage? Why? *(the horses; She loves horses and is good at riding them. She also likes Vern, who is in charge of the stables. pp. 6–7)*

3. What do the names Vern gives the horses tell the reader about Vern's life? *(He was a slave on a plantation, but with the help of kind people, he escaped from slavery, made his way north, and eventually became a free man. pp. 7–8)*

4. Why do you think Charlotte and Hayward spend time dreaming about the future? *(Answers will vary. Suggestion: They have no family, so they only have each other. Dreaming of a happy future gives them hope.)*

5. Why had Charlotte quit lining up when a couple came to look for a child? *(Most couples only wanted boys. Also, Mrs. Boyle didn't want anyone to adopt Charlotte because she would lose her kitchen help. p. 19)*

6. Do you agree or disagree with Mrs. Boyle's actions when she told a couple who hoped to adopt Charlotte that they could not adopt her because Charlotte was her niece? Why? *(Answers will vary. p. 19)*

7. Why do you think Charlotte tries not to cry, even when she finds out Freedom has passed away? *(Answers will vary. p. 24)*

8. Do you agree or disagree with Mr. Millshark's decision not to let Charlotte ride horses or work in the stables any longer? Why or why not? *(Answers will vary. Suggestion: disagree; Horses are the one happiness Charlotte has at the orphanage. p. 26)*

9. How do you think Hayward felt when he found out he was getting adopted? *(Answers will vary. Suggestions: excited, nervous, happy, relieved, loved. p. 27)*

10. What are all of the causes that lead Charlotte to make the decision to leave the orphanage? *(She is forbidden to work with the horses, Freedom dies, Hayward gets adopted, and she is ordered to work in the kitchen with Mrs. Boyle full-time. Without a best friend, her horses, or any hope of being adopted, Charlotte doesn't see any reason to stay at the orphanage. pp. 22–27)*

11. **Prediction:** What is Charlotte's plan? Will she be able to successfully escape from the orphanage?

Supplementary Activities

1. History: Research the Underground Railroad and determine whether or not Vern might have used it to escape to the north.

2. Writing: Write a letter that Hayward might have written to Charlotte had she stayed at the orphanage. Then write a letter that Charlotte might have sent Hayward in return.

3. Geography: Look at a map of the United States. Find New Hampshire and then Worcester, Massachusetts. Calculate the distance that Charlotte traveled when she ran away from the orphanage.

4. Literary Analysis: Begin the Story Map on page 10 of this guide. Add to the map as you read.

5. Character Analysis: Begin the Character Attribute Web on page 11 of this guide for Charlotte. Add to the web as you read.

Chapters 3–5, pp. 32–65

Charlotte, with Vern's help, escapes from the orphanage by posing as a young man. After a stagecoach ride to Worcester, Massachusetts, she finds a job working as a stable boy. The owner then offers "Charley" a job driving stagecoaches when he moves his business to Rhode Island.

Vocabulary

- molasses (34)
- furrows (36)
- intentions (37)
- plumped (39)
- crudely (40)
- locks (41)
- makeshift (41)
- traces (45)
- varnish (45)
- droning (47)
- lofts (51)
- mucking (56)
- reliable (56)
- winced (58)
- cocky (59)
- reins (61)
- exhilaration (64)

Discussion Questions

1. Who does Charlotte get to help her run away? How do these people help her? *(Hayward: he brings her clothes; Vern: he gives her information, scissors, and money, pp. 39–40)*

2. Do you approve of Vern assisting Charlotte in running away from the orphanage? Why or why not? *(Answers will vary.)*

3. What does Charlotte do to change her appearance? Why does she do this? *(She cuts her hair and puts on Hayward's clothes so she looks like a boy. She does this so she won't be recognized. Also, people will not suspect a boy walking alone, but seeing a girl alone would arouse suspicion. p. 41)*

4. What does Charlotte do to "make it look like different things could have happened" (pp. 41–43)? Do you think people will believe she may have drowned? *(She hangs her apron on a tree branch by the river. Answers will vary.)*

5. Why does Charlotte stare at the woman in the coach who asks Charlotte what her name is? *(She is pretending to be a boy but hasn't thought about what her name would be yet. p. 46)*

6. Why does Charlotte now know what Vern meant when he said, "plants can't breathe and grow in a box that's too tight" (p. 47)? *(Answers will vary but should mention that, for Charlotte, the orphanage was a box that was too tight—it was suffocating her by keeping her from the things she loved. In the freedom of the city, she feels like anything is possible.)*

7. Why does Charlotte feel frightened and lonely once she gets off of the coach? *(She did not think about what she would do after she got away from the orphanage. In Manchester, she knows no one and has very little money. p. 49)*

8. Why does Charlotte offer to help the driver with his horses? What opportunity does helping the driver give her? *(because she feels safe around horses; the opportunity to sneak into the loft to sleep for the night, pp. 49–50)*

9. Why doesn't Charlotte tell Ebeneezer the truth when he finds her in the loft? Do you think he believes her story? *(Answers will vary. She doesn't know who he is or if he will return her to Mr. Millshark if he knows she is a runaway orphan. pp. 57–59)*

10. Why does Ebeneezer ask "Charley" about the girl who is missing from the orphanage? Do you think he knows "Charley" is really a girl? Why or why not? *(Answers will vary. He probably does suspect that "Charley" is the girl who escaped from the orphanage. pp. 57–58)*

11. Why does Ebeneezer let Charlotte attempt to drive a six-in-the-hand coach? *(He knows she needs a job, and he can only think of one other person who could work with horses the way she can. He wants her to move with him to Rhode Island and work for him driving coaches there. pp. 59–60)*

12. What do Charlotte's attempts to drive the six-in-the-hand say about her character? *(Answers will vary. Suggestion—It shows she is desperate to stay away from the orphanage, but also that she has courage and doesn't like to give up.)*

Supplementary Activities

1. Writing: Write a poem or a short story about a stable hand who takes care of horses. Use vocabulary that a stable hand would use to describe actual stables and horses.

2. Writing: Write a page that Charlotte might have written in a diary the day that Ebeneezer asks her about the girl who is missing from the orphanage. Include thoughts Charlotte might have had during her conversation with Ebeneezer and as she spent time learning to drive the six-in-the-hand.

3. Art: Draw a picture of a stagecoach attached to six horses. Then draw a picture of Charlotte dressed as Charley driving the team.

In the Middle–Chapter 7, pp. 67–92

Charlotte, known as Charley, earns a reputation of being the best stagecoach driver on the Atlantic coast. One day, she has the pleasure of carrying Mr. Millshark in her coach, and after giving him an adventurous ride, she takes his boots to give to Ebeneezer. Then she travels to the Pacific coast where she hopes to one day buy a ranch of her own.

Discussion Questions

1. Now that Charlotte is 18, why can't she reveal her true identity? *(She is still a woman doing a man's job. If people thought she was a woman, they wouldn't let her drive a stagecoach. p. 69)*

2. Why is Charlotte so startled one morning when she sees the list of passengers she will be transporting? *(Mr. Millshark is on the list. She knows if he recognizes her, he will tell everyone she is a woman, and no one will want to ride with her again. p. 71)*

3. How does Ebeneezer respond to Charlotte when she says she doesn't think she can drive? What does this say about Ebeneezer's character? *(Ebeneezer recognizes Mr. Millshark as the man who came looking for a lost girl from the orphanage years ago. He probably knows "Charley" is that lost girl, and that she is afraid of getting caught. Instead of being rude, he encourages Charlotte by reminding her that she is the boss and has great skill in driving horses. Answers will vary. This episode shows Ebeneezer to be a compassionate man who is also wise and kind. p. 72)*

Vocabulary
coddle (68)
precarious (68)
recognition (69)
manifest (70)
jittery (72)
reputable (73)
maneuvered (74)
rollicking (74)
mired (75)
bog (77)
untamed (80)
secured (81)
bullion (83)
livery (84)
delta (85)
disembarked (86)

4. Why does Charlotte enjoy having power over Mr. Millshark? What does she do with her "power"? Do you agree or disagree with Charlotte's actions? *(She enjoys having power because he had so much power over her for so many years. Because she can, Charlotte takes the coach through a muddy bog so it will get stuck, and Mr. Millshark has to get muddy to help her free the coach. Answers will vary. pp. 75–77)*

5. Do you think it was right or fair of Charlotte to hide Mr. Millshark's fancy boots so she could give them to Ebeneezer? Why or why not? *(Answers will vary. pp. 77–78)*

6. Why does the talk about land interest Charlotte when approached with a job offer from Stevens and Birch? *(She has always dreamed of owning her own ranch.)*

7. What is Ebeneezer's reaction to Charlotte's leaving? Why does he have this reaction? *(He is very critical of her decision. He does not want her to go. Answers will vary. Suggestions: He is afraid something will happen to her. He doesn't want to lose his best driver. pp. 82–83)*

8. Who interests Charlotte once she arrives in California? Why does she think this person is brave? Do you think Charlotte considers herself brave? *(a woman handing out handbills and talking about women's right to vote; because she is standing in front of a group of jeering men; Answers will vary. pp. 87–89)*

9. **Prediction:** Will Charlotte survive in the West? Will she be able to buy a ranch?

Supplementary Activities

1. History: Research the California Gold Rush. Try to find specific information about Sacramento, California, and what it means to be a "boomtown."

2. Math/Science/History: Calculate how long it would take you to travel from Rhode Island to California today by car or plane. Then compare that length of time to one month, the length of time it would have taken Charlotte to travel there. Have a class discussion about the pros and cons of the advancing technology of transportation.

Chapter 8–In the End, pp. 93–134

Charlotte gets kicked in the face by a wild horse, causing her to go blind in one eye. She continues to drive stagecoaches, and after saving the lives of some passengers, becomes a famous driver. After buying a ranch, she receives a visit from Hayward and becomes the first woman to vote in a presidential election. In the end, Ebeneezer joins Charlotte in California.

Discussion Questions

1. What does the doctor discover about Charlotte? What else does he tell her that relates to his discovery? *(that she is a woman; that she is not the only woman pretending to be a man, pp. 94–95)*

2. How do you think Charlotte feels when the doctor tells her she may never be able to see again in her left eye? How would you feel if you were in her situation? *(Answers will vary.)*

Vocabulary
shod (93)
churned (93)
self-conscious (96)
weathered (98)
embankment (101)
reluctantly (103)
portly (105)
jibbed (107)
clamoring (107)
rancid (110)
corrals (111)
mortgage (112)
quandary (112)
hitched (125)
banter (127)
qualified (129)
colt (134)

3. What does Charlotte decide to do though she can only see with one eye? Do her actions surprise you? Why or why not? *(She decides to teach herself how to drive a stagecoach with only one good eye. She also learns how to depend more on her other senses. Answers will vary. Suggestion: Her actions are not surprising. She has always been determined to succeed at whatever she puts her mind to. pp. 99–103)*

4. Charlotte demands to have her driving tested regardless of the weather. Why does Charlotte want to be treated like any other driver? In what other parts of her life does Charlotte want to be treated equally? *(Charlotte wants to be measured with everyone else, regardless of her handicap. She wants to be able to drive at any time. At the same time, she wants to be recognized as a valuable driver and informed citizen even though she is a woman.)*

5. Consider the incident when Charlotte saves her passengers' lives. Do you think she was a better driver before she hurt her eye or now that she only has one good eye? Explain. *(Answers will vary. Suggestion: Her handicap has made her more careful. pp. 105–107)*

6. What does Charlotte learn from Margaret about some land for sale and about Margaret's property? What do you think she will do with this information? *(The land for sale is 25 acres with an apple orchard, some hens, and a front pasture that runs to the main road. Margaret's land is about to be taken away from her by the bank because she doesn't have enough money to make payments on it since her husband died. Answers will vary. pp. 110–112)*

7. Describe Hayward's visit with Charlotte. *(They are both happy to see each other and talk about what they've been doing. Hayward talks about his different jobs. Charlotte talks about making her property a way station. They reminisce about the orphanage and talk about how things there have changed. pp. 116–120)*

8. Why doesn't Charlotte agree to go with Hayward to get his parents? Do you agree or disagree with her decision? *(because she belongs at her new home and doesn't want to miss the upcoming elections; Answers will vary. pp. 122–123)*

9. How does Charlotte feel about her decision to vote? *(that she will be proving that a woman can make as sound a decision as a man can; She knows that one day people will discover she is a woman, and then they will remember how they looked up to her, a woman, as a respectable citizen; She also believes her vote is not just for her, but for all of the people in the country who are denied the right to vote. pp. 124, 129)*

10. While waiting to vote, many of the men make comments about a woman's right to vote. Do you agree or disagree with their points of view? *(Answers will vary. p. 127)*

11. What do you think of the names Charlotte gives her twin foals? Why do you think she chose these names? *(Answers will vary. Suggestion: She names one Vern's Thunder after the man who first introduced her to horses, and she named the other Freedom after the first horse she loved. p. 134)*

12. **Prediction:** Has Ebeneezer come to stay? Will Hayward ever return?

Supplementary Activities

1. History: Research the presidential race between Ulysses S. Grant and Horatio Seymour. Write a paragraph about what you learn about the election. In your paper, guess which candidate Charlotte voted for.

2. Science: Research to find out how common it is for a horse to have twins. Share your findings with the class.

3. Math: The land Charlotte bought is 25 acres. Determine approximately how much space 25 acres would cover in your neighborhood.

Post-reading Discussion Questions

1. Imagine what it would be like living your whole life as a different person. Would it be fun? hard? Then discuss whether or not you think it was fair that Charlotte could only have the life she wanted if people thought she was a man rather than a woman. Should she have tried to pursue her goals while letting people know her true identity? *(Answers will vary.)*

2. The author fabricated Charlotte's friendship with Hayward. Do you think it is realistic that Charlotte would have maintained a friendship from the orphanage after all of the traveling she did throughout her life? Why do you think so? *(Yes, because Charlotte was very dedicated. If she was able to keep her secret of being a woman for so many years, she probably would have been able to maintain communication with Hayward. Answers will vary.)*

3. Compare and contrast Charlotte and Hayward at the beginning of the story and at the end of the story. Specifically discuss whether or not they find families and how their "family life" affects them. *(Hayward is adopted, and so he is able to have a family. Charlotte's family consists of Ebeneezer and Hayward. Both at the beginning of the story and at the end, Charlotte and Hayward view each other as family.)*

4. How would the story be different if Charlotte hadn't had friends at the orphanage like Hayward and Vern? How important do you think it is to have good friends? *(Charlotte might not have come to love horses without Vern, and she probably would not have had the help she needed to escape from the orphanage. Vern and Hayward made her time at the orphanage bearable. Answers will vary.)*

5. Imagine how Charlotte's life would have been different if she had been a boy instead of a girl. Do you think her life should have been different as a boy? Why or why not? *(If Charlotte had been a boy, she might have been adopted. She also could have shown her love for horses and worked without hiding her true identity. Answers will vary.)*

6. Charlotte had a talent for working with horses. What other talents do you think she had that helped her to succeed? What talents do you have? *(She was determined to keep her secret, and she had a talent for never letting her guard down to others. Answers will vary.)*

7. In Charlotte's time, it was illegal for women to vote. Do you think it was right for Charlotte to break the law by voting in the presidential election? Why or why not? Is there ever a time when breaking the law is justified? *(Answers will vary.)*

8. How do you think the people in Charlotte's town felt when they found out she was a woman? How would you have felt if you had been in their place? *(They probably felt surprised that she could keep such a big secret from so many people. Answers will vary.)*

9. Discuss the theme of kindness and how people's acts of kindness move this story along. What other themes are evident in the story? Why do you think so? *(Vern's kindness to Charlotte allows her to discover her love of horses and allows her to escape from the orphanage. Ebeneezer allows Charlotte to work for him and stay in his loft. Other themes include bravery, courage, and determination. Answers will vary.)*

10. If Charlotte could have written down one piece of advice right before she died, what do you think she would have said? *(Answers will vary.)*

Post-reading Extension Activities

1. Have students write a persuasive essay telling fellow students why it is important to vote after they turn 18. Then, organize a campaign with the entire class to educate other students about why every vote is valuable in a democracy.

2. Lead students in a discussion about women's suffrage. Have students do research and pick a specific person or topic (i.e., voting rights, etc.) to be the topic of an oral report.

3. Have students chart each place Charlotte lived on a map of the United States. If possible, have students use a map that is an accurate representation of the country in the early 1800s.

4. Have students create a diorama of Charlotte leading a six-in-the-hand stagecoach.

5. Create a glossary of "horse words"—words used to describe horses and equipment used to ride them or take care of them. Include the words, their parts of speech, and their definitions.

6. Research a boomtown that existed in California during the Gold Rush days. Compare and contrast what the city was like then and now, if it still exists.

7. Make an eye-patch for yourself. Try to read, write, and walk around the classroom while wearing the eye-patch. Then write an essay explaining whether or not it was more difficult to function using only one eye. Be sure to give specific examples.

8. Charlotte tried to keep informed about the politics of where she lived. Find out something about politics in your area. Begin by finding out the names of your city's mayor, your state's governor, and your state's United States Congress representatives and senators. Decorate a poster board with the information. Attach pictures of the politicians, if possible, and note the political party to which they belong (Democrat, Republican, etc.).

9. In the story, Vern could not read. Pretend you are in charge of teaching someone how to read. Where would you begin? Outline a simple plan to teach someone the basics of reading. Be sure to include important elements like the alphabet and the sounds letters make.

10. Write a letter to Charlotte telling her what you think about her life (as it is portrayed in the book) and the decisions she made. You can also include any questions you would like to ask her if she were still alive.

11. Think about how women were treated when Chalotte lived compared to how women are treated today. Complete the Venn Diagram on page 12 of this guide.

12. Write a riddle for one of the characters in the book using the Who Am I? graphic on page 13 of this guide.

13. Think about how parts of the book affected you in different ways. Complete the Effects of Reading graphic on page 14 of this guide.

Assessment for *Riding Freedom*

Assessment is an ongoing process. The following ten items can be completed during the novel study. Once finished, the student and teacher will check the work. Points may be added to indicate the level of understanding.

Name _____ Date _____

Student	Teacher	
_____	_____	1. Write a review of the book. Include your opinion about whether or not you think other students should read *Riding Freedom*.
_____	_____	2. Write one more chapter to the book. Include what happens to Charlotte, Ebeneezer, and Hayward.
_____	_____	3. Complete one of the Post-reading Extension Activities (see page 22 of this guide). Present the assignment to the class.
_____	_____	4. Write an essay that explains one of Charlotte's decisions during the course of the book. Describe what Charlotte's options were and why she made the decision she did.
_____	_____	5. Create a collage that depicts Charlotte's character.
_____	_____	6. Choose one character from the book who had a significant impact on Charlotte's life. Draw a picture of the character and write a short paragraph explaining what role s/he played in Charlotte's life story.
_____	_____	7. Write a short essay explaining why you think the book is titled *Riding Freedom*. Then brainstorm other possible titles for the book.
_____	_____	8. Correct any quizzes or tests taken over the book.
_____	_____	9. Select one of Charlotte's character traits. Write a poem or song that gives examples of Charlotte demonstrating this character trait.
_____	_____	10. On a map, indicate all of the places Charlotte lived throughout her life. Then, for each place she lived, write a sentence or two explaining why she came there and, if applicable, why she left.

Linking Novel Units® Lessons to National and State Reading Assessments

During the past several years, an increasing number of students have faced some form of state-mandated competency testing in reading. Many states now administer state-developed assessments to measure the skills and knowledge emphasized in their particular reading curriculum. The discussion questions and post-reading questions in this Novel Units® Teacher Guide make excellent open-ended comprehension questions and may be used throughout the daily lessons as practice activities. The rubric below provides important information for evaluating responses to open-ended comprehension questions. Teachers may also use scoring rubrics provided for their own state's competency test.

Please note: The Novel Units® Student Packet contains optional open-ended questions in a format similar to many national and state reading assessments.

Scoring Rubric for Open-Ended Items

3-Exemplary
- Thorough, complete ideas/information
- Clear organization throughout
- Logical reasoning/conclusions
- Thorough understanding of reading task
- Accurate, complete response

2-Sufficient
- Many relevant ideas/pieces of information
- Clear organization throughout most of response
- Minor problems in logical reasoning/conclusions
- General understanding of reading task
- Generally accurate and complete response

1-Partially Sufficient
- Minimally relevant ideas/information
- Obvious gaps in organization
- Obvious problems in logical reasoning/conclusions
- Minimal understanding of reading task
- Inaccuracies/incomplete response

0-Insufficient
- Irrelevant ideas/information
- No coherent organization
- Major problems in logical reasoning/conclusions
- Little or no understanding of reading task
- Generally inaccurate/incomplete response